CHRISTMAS TREES
AND HOLIDAY GREENS

Also by these authors

101 Commonsense Gardening Tips

CHRISTMAS TREES AND HOLIDAY GREENS

Decorating Ideas from *The Common Sense Gardener*™

MICHAEL *and* DEBORAH SWEETON

PHOTOGRAPHS BY MICHAEL SWEETON

THE LYONS PRESS
Guilford, Connecticut

AN IMPRINT OF THE GLOBE PEQUOT PRESS

The Lyons Press is an imprint of The Globe Pequot Press.

10 9 8 7 6 5 4 3 2 1

Printed in the United States of America

Text design by Casey Shain

ISBN 1-59228-053-6

Library of Congress Cataloging-in-Publication data is available on file.

DEDICATION

Once in everyone's life there passes a special person who changes and enriches all they touch. David Barber was such a person. Dave's enthusiasm for horticulture was evident to everyone who met him and his knowledge of plants, especially perennials, was without equal. Dave was our partner, colleague, and friend. He inspired us to pursue our dream of sharing our gardening knowledge with others through our books and television program. Though Dave passed away suddenly this year he lives in the pages of this book as well in our hearts.

CONTENTS

INTRODUCTION

here is no more exciting time than the Christmas season. Who doesn't approach this time of year bursting with anticipation of the wonders ahead? The smell of fresh-baked gingerbread, trudging through the snow to pick your perfect tree, or the decorating of your home with fresh greens and shiny ornaments, are all memories that evoke the holidays, and for many of us herald the most joyous time of the year.

For you, the gardener, the season doesn't have to end with the first falling snowflake. You can easily extend your season by "greening up" your outside planters and starting some narcissus bulbs in pots for holiday enjoyment. Scouring your neighborhood for the perfect Christmas tree, or meandering through your favorite greenhouse in search of a fresh poinsettia, is all part of creating a special holiday memory. If you've ever had trouble creating any of these memories, or been frustrated by just not knowing how to get started, we're here to help.

You do not have to be an artistic genius or an outdoor expert to expand your gardening hobby into the holiday season. In the pages that follow we'll take

you step-by-step on the journey, to the perfect gardener's holiday season. So pour yourself a nice cup of hot chocolate, curl up by the fire, and begin your journey by turning the page.

CHRISTMAS TREES
AND HOLIDAY GREENS

PLANTS of the SEASON

What would the holidays be without live plants, greens, and flowers? Flowers and plants pick up our spirits when we're stressed, make wonderful, inexpensive gifts for friends, and provide a festive "home sweet home" atmosphere. In the pages that follow we will introduce you to the most popular houseplants for the holiday season, and give you some common sense tips for their care.

While poinsettias are the definitive Christmas flower, there are many other plants that help brighten the holiday season. Whether you are a "do-it-yourselfer," or want a ready-to-display beauty, the following choices will make your holiday special.

While poinsettias are the definitive Christmas flower, there are many other plants that help brighten the holiday season.

Poinsettia — the Christmas Flower:

Legend has it that a poor Mexican girl named Pepita was on her way to see the baby Jesus. She did not have a gift to bring, so she stopped along the road and picked some weeds and as she made her way to the manger the plants began to turn red. When she arrived, her plain weeds had become a beautiful gift of *Flores de Noche Buena*, flowers of the Holy Night; now called poinsettias. What a wonderful story, mixing fact with fiction. Poinsettias are photoperiodic, that is, they change their bract color when the days gradually become shorter. You can almost picture this young girl making the long journey and having such a miracle occur. Believe it or not, this story captures what poinsettias have come to mean in our society—the perfect holiday present!

The poinsettia is now the number one selling potted plant in the United States.

There is a myth we do need to dispel, however, if you want to truly enjoy your holiday poinsettia. The old wives' tale that these plants are poisonous has been around since the early 1900s, a fallacy brought about by the report of a little child who fell ill after eating poinsettias. This was never proven to be true, yet year after year the story keeps getting recycled through general interest magazines, scaring a new generation. Much research has been done, led by Ohio State University. These studies have shown that poinsettias are NOT poisonous, and that you would have to ingest so many to feel ill that your neighborhood grower would be completely sold out! It is recommended, however, that you do not let children and pets eat them, since the latex they contain, when ingested in large amounts, can cause stomach irritation.

Do you know where poinsettias originated? Our opening story about Pepita should have given you a hint. Poinsettias (*Euphorbia pulcherrima*) are from the tropical climate of Mexico. The first US ambassador to Mexico was a man named Joel Poinsett whose home was Charleston, South Carolina. In 1825, on one of his trips through the Mexican countryside, Ambassador Poinsett became enamored of this brilliant scarlet flower. He brought some of these beautiful winter-blooming plants back to the United States when his service was over. Since that time the poinsettia has grown immensely in popularity, so that it is now the number one selling potted plant in the US. There was only the familiar red color in the beginning, but through selective breeding and natural mutation we now enjoy a wide variety of colors and forms. Before we discuss these varieties

The leaves, called "bracts," are actually what display the coloration, and in the center of the colored leaves is the true flower, which is yellow and is called the cyathia.

you will need to have a little botany lesson.

Did you know that the parts of the poinsettia that turn color are not the flower at all? The leaves, called "bracts," are actually what display the coloration, and in the center of the colored leaves is the true flower, which is yellow and is called the cyathia. When choosing a poinsettia to purchase for your home or as a gift it is important to know that the plant should still have its cyathia. Cyathia loss can indicate that the poinsettia is old, or that it has been exposed to poor conditions, such as cold, or drying of the soil (see our care instructions below) prior to being put out on display. If you purchase a poinsettia lacking this true flower you are headed for trouble. The plant won't last as long, you'll think it is your fault, and will probably never buy another of these attractive plants. This is not a good thing for those of us who make our living growing plants!

You have probably noticed that in the past twenty years there has been an amazing increase in breeding programs in an effort to develop new colors and forms of the poinsettia. There are now hundreds of varieties. Even within the reds, the range runs from scarlet, to dark red, to cranberry. There are several shades of white and cream, many different pinks, coral, bicolor, speckled, and even purples and burgundy. And if

Some of the various new colors and forms of the poinsettia— Jingle Bells, *top;* marble, middle; *plum,* bottom.

color choice wasn't enough, the past few years have witnessed new varieties being developed that produce wavy or curly bracts. Of course plain red wouldn't do here either, so these new types are now becoming available in other colors as well. There are a few varieties that we have come to recognize as definite winners in terms of retaining their freshness in the less than ideal conditions in which they often find themselves. For a red selection, we have found Red Velvet to be an exceptional performer, maintaining its color and leaves for several months even under medium-light conditions. Snowcap takes the prize for a white, with true white-colored bracts that do not fade to a creamy yellow, and also has the ability to hold its cyathia (remember, that's the true flower) for a month or more. Other must haves include Nutcracker, especially the pink variety, and Jingle Bells, a speckled red and white in the novelty category. Now you have no excuse: No matter what your color scheme, you can join in the fun of celebrating the holidays with the quintessential "Christmas flower."

When purchasing a poinsettia to beautify your home for the season, there are a few important things to remember. In most cases you should buy a poinsettia from someone with the knowledge of how they are grown and cared for, such as a garden center or florist. You will be more successful, since the plant will be likely

In addition to shades including white and cream, new varieties are being developed that produce wavy or curly bracts, as shown below.

to last well past the holiday season. Poinsettias are tropical plants that need warm temperatures, and many of the stores where poinsettias are now available do not provide optimal conditions, with their low light and drafty doorways. Poinsettias do not tolerate adverse conditions such as lack of sufficient light, cold drafts, and over- or underwatering. Be mindful of the fact that a plant exposed to these conditions will not last as long as if you had purchased one that had been given the proper care.

How do I care for my poinsettia after I get it home? This is an excellent question, and one the little care tags that come with your plant sometimes fail to explain clearly. Here are some simple tips. If the temperature was below 50 degrees when you bought your poinsettia, it should have had a paper or plastic sleeve around it to protect it on the ride home. This is critical, as poinsettias

will not tolerate temperatures below that mark. If you live in a region of the country that can experience very cold temperatures in December, you have to be mindful of this tip. If it is below freezing outside when you are taking your poinsettia home, ideally the car should be warmed up first. Even the ten-minute ride home in below-freezing temperatures can severely damage, or even kill your new purchase!

Once safely home, cut the sleeve off the plant, and check to see if the soil in the pot is dry. Put a small amount of soil between your fingers and feel it. If it is light, fluffy, and you can't detect any moisture, then the soil is dry. Although many attempts have been made to quantify "dry" soil, it is still not an exact science; you have to get your fingers dirty and use common sense. A good exercise is to take a cup of the soil mix you typically use, let it dry out

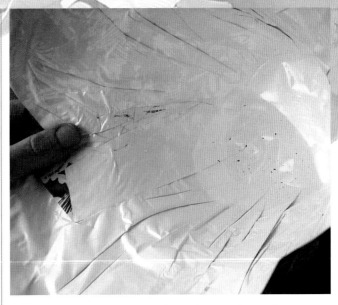

Be sure to cut a hole in the foil, or remove it altogether and place the pot on a saucer.

spread evenly on a sheet of wax paper for three or four days, then thoroughly water half of it. Now you can compare what wet soil and dry soil feel like. Each day for the next few days feel the wet half as it dries, and you will get a real sense of how to care for any plant. Having said all that, if your poinsettia is dry water it thoroughly, completely wetting the soil. Remember, many of the plants you buy have foil or pot covers as decorations, and these do not provide drainage, which results in your plant sitting in water. Just as you would get sick with your feet sitting in water all the time, your poinsettia will quickly suffer from these same conditions. Be sure to cut a hole in the foil, or remove it altogether, and place the pot on a saucer. This will allow the water to drain away from the roots. Check every other day to see if it needs water, and water if the soil is slightly dry to the touch. Poinsettias are not tolerant of "wet feet" or constantly soggy soil. Under these conditions the leaves will turn yellow and drop. After a while the plant will look as if it is dry and wilted, when actually what has occurred is a condition known as root rot. The roots, deprived of oxygen, have actually turned to mush, and can no longer absorb water. This is to be avoided at all costs. On the other hand, poinset-

Poinsettias are not tolerant of "wet feet," or constantly soggy soil. Under these conditions the leaves will turn yellow and drop.

tias also cannot tolerate their soil becoming too dry. The plant won't die, but the leaves will also turn yellow and fall off. I think we can all agree a plant's beauty is diminished when it reaches this point, and that you certainly are not going to get your money's worth! During the few weeks of Christmas the plant does not have to have direct sun; it can be placed anywhere in your home for maximum enjoyment. However, after the holiday, if you want to keep your plant healthy, you will need to move it to a sunny window. This should be a window that gets at least six to eight hours of sun per day, which generally is any window with a southern exposure. Remember that poinsettias are tropical plants and therefore require warm temperatures in the home. The ideal temperature should be 60 to 70 degrees, and you must avoid drafty locations at all costs.

After the holiday, if you want to keep your plant healthy, you will need to move it to a sunny window.

Poinsettias should also not be placed too close to a heater or fireplace, as this can cause them to dry out too quickly.

How do I get my plant to bloom again next year? It is not terribly hard; all you need is the right light and lots of patience. Any window that faces south, and which receives eight or more hours of direct sunlight per day, can provide the preferred southern exposure. Your poinsettia should retain its colored bracts well into spring in this type of location when it receives loving care. In mid-spring you can trim the plant back by one quarter to half its present height. If you like, you can place the plant outdoors (as long as the temperatures never fall below 55 degrees) and throughout the summer grow it outside in light shade. This is actually better for this vigorously growing plant, and it will produce a much bushier, well-branched specimen.

You can begin to fertilize using 20-20-20 or 20-10-20 mix, at a rate of one teaspoon per gallon of water, every second or third watering. Remember from our first book *101 Commonsense Gardening Tips*, that these three numbers refer respectively to the ratio of nitrogen, phosphorus, and potassium in the mixture. Nitrogen promotes leaf growth; phosphorus encourages the production of flowers; and potassium is essential for strong root growth. Because poinsettias are such vigorous growers they will need these nutrients to maximize their growth.

At the beginning of June, check the roots to see if the plant needs to be repotted. If it appears to be pot-bound then transplant to the next size pot using a good commercial potting soil like Sunshine Mix®. A plant is pot-bound (or root-bound) when its roots have become so numerous that they have filled up all

In mid-spring you can trim the plant back by one quarter to half its present height.

the available air space in the soil. This condition hinders nutrient uptake by the poinsettia, thus hastening the plant's decline. A good way to tell that your plant is becoming root-bound is that it needs more frequent watering, often every day. At the beginning of August, you should cut the plant back to three to four leaves per stem. This will insure that you will get many flowers (actually colored bracts) and after all, isn't that the whole point? Remember to move your poinsettia indoors if night-time temperatures in your area go below 50 degrees. Also, remember that poinsettias are photoperiodic, which means they only bloom when there are a certain number of hours of darkness each day. To encourage this development, starting in mid-September, you will have to place the plant in a sunny spot during the day, and in a darkened room at night. If that is not possible, then you can move it to a closet every evening, or cover it with a black bag around 5 PM each night. You will need to continue this regimen until the end of November. By then, if you have done this consistently, you will have produced colored bracts, and flowers! Remember, your home is not like a greenhouse, so it will be difficult for you to get your poinsettia to look quite as nice a one grown professionally, but it is fun to see the process!

Now that you are an expert in taking care of your poinsettia, let's get to your creative side. When decorating your home with poinsettias, there are some fun things to try. You can make a pretty display by placing three different colors together in a grouping, achieving a tricolor effect. You can use any container, but we prefer Christmas baskets with small pots placed inside for a cute holiday touch. We have even used an old fruit crate that is incredibly charming

Covering the poinsettia with a black bag each night will help produce colored bracts and flowers. Decorative planters make nice holiday decorations.

when stuffed with poinsettias and greens. Another idea, which only takes about ten minutes, is to dress up your large pot with greens. You can cut white pine branches—or any green you like—into lengths of about 12 to 18 inches. Place them directly into the soil around the base of the plant. Add a bow, and *voilà*, a dressed-up poinsettia!

Amaryllis (Hippeastrum)

There are alternatives to poinsettias, if you would prefer not to have one in your home. Let's start with one of the most elegant offerings from the plant kingdom, the amaryllis (*Hippeastrum* hybrid). Nothing says Christmas for some people like an amaryllis. This is a tropical bulbous herb, and there are over seventy species, with many more hybrids. A species refers to a naturally occurring amaryllis. A hybrid is the result of breeding two different varieties or colors of amaryllis, producing an entirely unique variety. Here in the United States we are most familiar with the Dutch hybrids, although in recent years we have been lucky to find South American and South African bulbs in many local garden centers. These bulbs are generally larger than their Dutch cousins and they produce multiple flower stalks. We have become particularly fond of

Nothing says Christmas for some people like an Amaryllis. Starting one from a bulb is easy.

Apple Blossom (white with pink veins); Candy Floss (a vivid pink); and Double Six (a new red, which is brilliant). These are all South African varieties and well worth searching for.

Starting an amaryllis from a bulb is easy. These are readily available during the fall at most garden retailers. Choose a large, firm bulb and a tall pot that is an inch or two bigger in diameter than the bulb itself. Place the bulb in the soil so that ¼ inch of it remains exposed above the top of the soil. Water thoroughly and place the pot in a warm spot, preferably at 70 degrees or more. Let the soil get dry to the touch before watering your amaryllis again. In the home environment it will take about eight weeks from the time you plant the bulb until it flowers. Once the leaves and flower stalk have emerged, and the bud has swollen, keep the soil moist so that the amaryllis won't wilt;

wilting shortens flower life. Cover the soil with decorative sheet moss, the finishing touch on the perfect Christmas flower.

Have you had amaryllis before but were never successful in getting them to flower again the following year? It's easy to rebloom your amaryllis if you follow a few commonsense gardening steps. While it is still blooming, keep the soil moist but not soggy. Once it has finished flowering, cut the stalk at the base—but do not cut the leaves—and continue watering and fertilizing occasionally with houseplant fertilizer, until midsummer. Now move the pot to a cool, dry, dark spot. Forget about it until late October or early November. Cut off any remaining leaves at this point and place the pot in a sunny, warm location. Start watering, as before, and in about six weeks you'll have blooms again.

Once the amaryllis has finished flowering, cut the stalk at the base, above. Below, paper-white bulbs are available beginning in late September at your local garden center or nursery.

Paper-White (Narcissus)

Paper-whites (*Narcissus*), belonging to the amaryllis family, are chiefly bulbous plants with twenty-five to thirty species, most quite fragrant. Narcissus are named for the mythological boy, so fond of his own reflection in a pool that he was magically changed into a flower. When you fall under the spell of the incredibly fragrant paper-whites you will certainly understand this fable. Paper-white bulbs are available beginning in late September at your local garden center or nursery. They are to be forced indoors, and many people plant them to enjoy just for the holidays. The term forcing refers to the fact that you are artificially creating the environment best suited for the growth and flowering of the bulbs when those conditions do not naturally exist. This allows us to enjoy plants that are not native to our area, or at a time when they would not normally bloom.

Planting paper-white bulbs is easy. Most containers are suitable. We prefer ones with good drainage, although these are one of the few plants that can be grown in a *cache pot*, an ornamental container of terra cotta or china, that doesn't necessarily provide drainage. Odd numbers of bulbs look best, and they should be almost touching each other for maximum effect. For example, five bulbs of 12/14 size (note: this refers to centimeters of bulb size, a common reference wherever bulbs are sold) in a 6 to 7 inch pot will give you a wonderful display. Place in potting soil or gravel, with the very top of the bulb sticking out. Water in and watch out! Try storing extra bulbs in the refrigerator and planting a few pots every couple of weeks. You'll have flowers all winter. Paper-whites are also a lovely flower-

Odd numbers of bulbs look best, and they should be almost touching each other for maximum effect.

ing plant to have on display for your New Year's Eve celebration.

After your paper-whites are planted, keep them in a bright or sunny location. This will prevent them from "stretching," and falling over. Stretching is when the plant stems elongate due to insufficient light which causes them to develop weak, thin stems. You will want to avoid this, as nothing can be more frustrating than to have your holiday paper-whites ruined. It will take four to six weeks in the home environment and then your paper-whites will start to bloom. Once they begin to flower, the cooler the area they're in, the longer the flowers will last. Keep the soil barely moist, not wet, especially if using a pot with no drainage. If your stems get to be too tall and tip over, don't worry—some green string or curling ribbon tied around all the stems about half way up will solve this problem.

Christmas Cactus
(*Schlumbergera bridgesii*)

The Christmas cactus (*Schlumbergera bridgesii*) and Thanksgiving cactus (*Schlumbergera truncate*) represent some of the easiest of the holiday plants to care for. Most of the newer varieties are among the Thanksgiving types. They have a slightly different leaf, mostly smooth with rounded edges, and come in many colors, ranging from brilliant pink to a golden yellow. A true Christmas cactus has a deep red flower, and a specific leaf shape which is more serrated along the leaf edge.

They prefer very bright light indoors, and can be allowed to go dry between waterings. During spring and summer they should be fertilized as your other houseplants are—at least once a month while they are actively growing. They can be placed outdoors in light shade when the night temperatures are

Christmas cacti represent some of the easiest of the holiday plants to care for. Below, watch carefully for tiny buds forming sometime around October 1.

above 50 degrees. They also can be kept indoors all year if you prefer.

How do you get Grandma's old Christmas cactus to bloom again? All holiday cacti (*Schlumbergera spp.*) can be forced to bloom at any time of year if you learn their requirements. They generally set buds when they are exposed to a combination of shorter days and cooler temperatures. In addition, dry soil conditions also have the effect of initiating bud formation, or bud "set," as it is often referred to by your more learned plant friends. However don't be intimidated by these plant aficionados, because you too can force your cactus into bloom. Starting about August 1, place the cactus in a cool but sunny window, and let the soil dry out well between waterings. Watch carefully for tiny buds forming sometime around October 1. After sighting buds, make sure the soil stays evenly moist, though not soaking wet, at all times. This is critical because letting the plant dry out now will cause your cactus's hard-earned buds to fall off. Fertilize at least once after the buds have formed. In about a month (mid-November), you'll have a spectacular display of flowers to kick off the holiday season.

Cyclamen (Cyclamen persicum or Cyclamen purpurascens)

Cyclamen (*Cyclamen persicum* or *C. purpurascens*) have become another very popular winter season plant from Thanksgiving all the way through New Years Day and beyond. They come in many colors, ranging from red and white (great for Christmas decorating) to a multitude of pinks, salmon, purple, and even magenta. Cyclamen come as either miniatures (*C. persicum* dwarf) or standard size, making them suitable for any decorating scheme. A miniature rarely exceeds 6 to 8 inches in height with correspondingly sized flowers, perfect for that nook or cranny spot. The standard size cyclamen generally

Cyclamen have become another very popular winter season plant.

grow to 10 to 12 inches in height, with a comparable spread. They make a wonderful table centerpiece that will brighten any winter day.

Caring for your cyclamen is easy. In the home setting, cyclamen like cool, bright conditions. Place your plant in an east or west window which will provide approximately five to six hours of sun per day. Allow the soil to become slightly dry before watering. Water thoroughly, let the pot drain, and don't provide water until the soil goes slightly dry again. When entertaining, you can move your cyclamen to the table as your arrangement, or wherever else you need instant beauty. Don't leave it in low-light conditions for very long, as its leaves will turn yellow and it will stop flowering. Prolonged time in low light conditions will eventually cause your cyclamen to just give up and die. Overwatering cyclamen also causes yellow leaves and eventual

Cyclamen come as either miniatures (C. persicum dwarf) or standard size, making them suitable for any decorating scheme.

death. Properly cared for, cyclamen will last for many months, while continuing to bloom. Many times cyclamen don't make it through the summer; it is simply too hot for them in most areas of the US. They come from a climate where the summers are cooler than ours. Don't fret, though; you can always get another when fall season arrives once again! If you are determined to attempt to keep your cyclamen from season to season, here are few helpful instructions. After it stops flowering and you can see no new buds under the foliage, begin to reduce the frequency of your waterings, letting the soil become a little drier each time. When all the leaves turn yellow, let the soil completely dry out. Put the pot in a cool, dry place, such as your basement, for the rest of the summer. When fall arrives—sometime after Labor Day— place your cyclamen back in a brightly lit area, water thoroughly, and keep the soil slightly moist until you begin to see leaves develop. From the point you see these first leaves emerge, keep the soil evenly moist, that is, neither too wet nor too dry. The key is to avoid extremes in soil moisture. If you have made it this far, chances are good you'll see flowers as winter begins.

Norfolk Island Pine (Araucaria heterophylla)

The Norfolk Island pine (*Araucaria heterophylla*) is native to Chile and Argentina and has become a popular, easy houseplant to care for. They are one of the few trees that are easy to grow inside when placed in front of a bright window. When purchasing one make sure there are four branches on each tier. Tiers are where side shoots or branches exit the main plant trunk. The tiers should be closely spaced, since this will ensure that as the tree grows in your home it

The Norfolk Island pine (Araucaria heterophylla) is native to Chile and Argentina and has become a popular, easy houseplant to care for.

will maintain a nice symmetrical appearance. Norfolk pines need to be kept evenly moist, as they will lose branches and needles if the soil is allowed to dry out too many times. The best thing about the Norfolk Island pine is the fact that it makes a great indoor living Christmas tree!

You can decorate it with lights and ornaments, provided they aren't too heavy. If you do use it as a tree, remember to move it back to its window after Christmas. Too much time spent in low light (less than six hours per day) will cause your pine to elongate, creating a lopsided, spindly appearance. It should be rotated one-quarter turn periodically to maintain symmetrical branch growth. While not fast growers, when kept in bright light Norfolk Island pines can reach 6 to 10 feet in height or more. They are a very distinguished addition to any home.

For many people holly is the green that most reminds them of Christmas.

Holly (Ilex)

For many people holly (*Ilex spp.*) is the green that most reminds them of Christmas. Most of what is used around the holidays are hybrid hollies, primarily from the species *cornuta* or *merserveae*. Both have serrated (or spiny) leaves, with four to eight

spines per leaf edge, or margin. One sprig of holly with some berries is a symbol instantly recognizable as heralding in the holidays. Holly, either the solid green variety or the variegated leaf type, is readily available from florists or garden centers during the Christmas season. Holly can be purchased as a potted plant at the holidays, but most of the time it is not suitable for outdoor planting in the colder parts of the US. These potted varieties are generally not tagged to tell you the species and to the untrained eye will be hard to identify. Your best bet would be to assume that it will not survive your winter and just enjoy it as a house plant. If your plans include outside planting after the season, ask for a named variety. We have found the *merserveae* species to be the best performers with Blue Maid a particular favorite for its hardiness, beautiful blue color, and abundance of berries. Speaking of berries, if your potted holly didn't come with berries, you can purchase artificial berries and attach them yourself. Most garden stores or nurseries carry bunches of these, which have attached wires for easy placement on the plant. Keep your potted holly in bright light, six or more hours per day, make sure the soil stays evenly moist, and enjoy this striking Christmas tradition.

Kalanchoes (Crassulaceae) are another traditional plant for winter. They have a succulent-type leaf which is thick and leathery.

Kalanchoe (Crassulaceae)

Kalanchoes (*Crassulaceae*) are another traditional plant for winter. They have a succulent-type leaf which is thick and leathery. A succulent generally has a long root system to maximize water uptake, and has also been designed by nature with thick stems and leaves which help the plant retain water, as well as minimize leaf evaporation. As succulents, kalanchoes are very tolerant of adverse conditions, which makes them very forgiving for the beginning gardener. Kalanchoes need direct sun to continue to bloom and thrive but they can go slightly dry between watering. They come in many colors, ranging from pink to orange to yellow to red. They are very long blooming, often lasting two or three months. When they have finished blooming, cut the old flower heads off. The plant will continue to grow, but make sure you let the soil dry completely between watering. Since they are in the succulent family they do not require much water. Your kalanchoe should flower again once fall approaches and the days begin to shorten.

There are so many alternatives everyone can join in the fun of gardening at the holidays. If you are a plant lover, or simply just want to impress your friends, there is a plant for you!

Displaying plants of the season makes the home more festive.

Left, an amaryllis with its stunning display of flowers.

Right, Norfolk Island Pines are sometimes called upside down trees.

Below, poinsettias can match any color scheme.

GREENS—
Fresh Cut for Inside

Tradition holds that the first use of greens to adorn the home was recorded in central Europe during the 1500s. We will never know exactly why, but can readily imagine families, facing the bleak prospect of a long winter, searching for ways to enjoy the sensory experiences of warmer times. What better—and relatively inexpensive—way than to bring a few boughs into a home that quickly fills with the distinct fragrance of fresh evergreens.

Whatever the origin of all the many decorating options for the holidays, dressing up our home interior with greens is our favorite. There are so many to choose from, allowing for many different colors and fragrances to fill your home. Using fresh live greens is an important

Whatever the origin of all the many decorating options for the holidays, dressing up our home interior with greens is our favorite.

Christmas tradition here, and around the world. This section will help you get the most from your fresh greens, either picked from your yard, or purchased at a garden center or from a florist.

Holly (Ilex)

Holly *(Ilex)* has to rank high on the list of plants that evoke thoughts of the Christmas season. There are a few important rules about caring for fresh-cut holly, and if you follow them you will enjoy it throughout the season. Most of the holly one can purchase as a cut green is from varieties that grow in areas of the country that do not see frigid temperatures, such as Oregon. Holly from these regions has large leaves and many berries, which makes it great for decorating. Unless you know the exact origin of the specimen, you have to assume it is not cold tolerant, and should only be used indoors. Holly that is not hardy in cold areas will turn brown fairly quickly and drop its leaves. If you want holly for outdoors, see our section that covers greens for outside, where we recommend holly native to your region or zone. Once you have purchased your fresh holly, you need to make a new cut on the stems, just as you would for fresh flowers. Use your garden pruners or shears, but dip them in a 10 percent solution of bleach and water. This will ensure

Cut the holly on a 45-degree angle, which facilitates water uptake by creating more surface area on the stem.

bacteria will not be introduced to the holly stems, resulting in poor water absorption. Make the cut on a 45-degree angle, which facilitates water uptake by creating more surface area on the stem. Place the stems in water immediately. You can enjoy the holly in a vase, or in an arrangement using floral foam, which is available from a florist or craft store. Holly will last for quite some time, especially if it is recut and the water changed every few days. It is quite likely that you can get your arrangement to last up to three to four weeks. Holly can be used out of water for short periods of time, but don't expect it to last more than five to seven days if used in this manner.

Boxwood (*Buxus spp.*)

Boxwood (*Buxus spp.*) is also very popular, especially for use in topiaries, wreaths, and arrangements, as well as roping or garland. There are many varieties, so be careful when purchasing it; some boxwood cannot be used outside for the same reason as holly, it may not be a variety that is hardy in your area. We prefer the *Buxus* hybrids Green Gem or Green Mountain for the northeast, or colder climates. If you are not sure whether it can safely be placed outdoors, ask your gardening professional to be sure. Boxwood is a small-leafed evergreen that is forest green in color. Some varieties have a distinct fragrance that some people don't care for; it has often been described as a "cat urine" smell. Test smell the tips first to see if it bothers you. It has an elegant Victorian look to it though, which is why it is so popular. Boxwood is easy to work with, cuts readily, and we have seen it last for as many as six to eight weeks if kept well watered in a vase or floral foam. Out of water, boxwood will dry but retains its leaves, so can still be used for decoration.

Boxwood is a small-leafed evergreen that is forest green in color.

Princess Pine (Lycopodium obscurum)

Princess pine (*Lycopodium obscurum*) is a small, soft-needled green usually found as roping or garland, but sometimes can also be found as a cut green for use in arrangements, or as a green around the house when left out of water. The name *Lycopodium* comes from the Greek *lukos* (wolf) and *podos* (foot) referring to this rhizomatous clubmoss's resemblance to a wolf's paw when observed growing along the ground. Princess pine is generally found in cool, damp, wooded thickets, in the vicinity of swamplands. Because of its natural habitat, the best way to keep it looking good for as long as possible is to soak the plant well, before using it, if it is not going to be placed in a vase or floral foam with water. We recommend soaking it in the sink or bathtub for at least half an hour, letting it dry, and only then using it to decorate. It is a beautiful green, especially when used as a soft accent or as the base of an arrangement. If properly soaked, and misted three times a week, it should last at least four weeks in your home.

White Pine (Pinus strobus)

White pine *(Pinus strobus)* has long, medium-green needles, and is used specifically because of its length and

White pine (Pinus strobus) *has long, medium-green needles, and is used specifically because of its length and the softening look this provides.*

the softening look this provides. White pine is widely used as a green indoors. It lasts about three weeks out of water, and is the least expensive of all the greens. It does shed, or lose its needles after several weeks, so that should be taken into consideration. It can be purchased as roping or garland, and in bunches either long or short. White pine does produce a fair amount of sap, a consideration when cutting it (wear gloves) and where you are placing it—avoiding furniture. It can be used in arrangements that are placed in water as well, where it will last longer, easily for an additional one to two weeks.

Juniper (Juniperus)

Juniper (*Juniperus*) is a bold choice, takes up a lot of space, has a bluish-green color, and is quite handsome with its prolific berries. There are many kinds of junipers and all have their place in decorating. Common juniper (*J. communis*), Chinese juniper (*J. chinensis*), and creeping juniper (*J. horizontalis*) are all varieties we have used. *Juniperus horizontalis* with its strikingly beautiful blue-green needles and blue berries is our favorite. It is a wonderful choice as a cut green and does well in water—lasting three to four weeks or longer, even if kept out of water.

Juniper (Juniperus) *is a bold choice, takes up a lot of space, has a bluish-green color, and is quite handsome with its prolific berries.*

What makes the junipers we have mentioned great candidates for decorating is their wide range of textures and shades. With needles of different lengths, and colors from dark green to yellowish green to blue, junipers all add variety with their unique qualities when incorporated with other more common greens, like balsam.

Cedar (Calocedrus spp.; Thuja spp.)

Cedars (*Calocedrus spp.; Thuja spp.*)—where to start! There are many beautiful cedars that can be used inside. We have two favorites; one is called incense cedar, which is beautifully soft with yellowish-brown cones at the tips. The other is western red cedar, which also has cones that are of miniature size. Cedar has a greenish-brown color, which is a nice contrast to all the other colors, and, since it has a brownish cast, when it starts to dry out it is not so noticeable. The needles don't fall off, like white pine, so it is a great choice as roping or as branches on a mantle. Red cedar is larger than incense cedar and makes a great garland. If you have never tried it, you should, as it is wonderful to work with and easy to keep looking fresh. To maximize its life, make sure to use clean, sharp pruners to put a fresh slanted cut on each branch before placing in water. If you plan to use cedar without water, just mist the greens two to three times per week to keep them looking their best.

Incorporating different types of greens in outdoor displays adds variety and texture, allowing you to express your creativity.

Regardless of what climate you live in, there is a wide variety of greens to choose from that will look good and last long in your outdoor display.

GREENS—
Fresh Cut for Outside

No holiday decorating is complete without incorporating fresh greens in your outside display. For centuries people have heralded the holiday season with sprigs of holly, or boughs of fresh-cut balsam. Festooned with bright swaths of cloth fashioned into a festive bow, or intermixed with brilliantly contrasting branches of white birch, an ordinary window box or planter can shout Merry Christmas to all! You can find a plentiful supply of greens at your local garden store, or you can look in your own backyard if you have an ample planting of evergreens. Be careful, however, of cutting too many branches from any tree growing in your yard, as improper or excessive pruning will cause the tree to become too sparse, reducing its effectiveness as screening. Follow our

No holiday decorating is complete without incorporating fresh greens in your outside display.

procedures in *101 Commonsense Gardening Tips* for proper pruning. Pay particular attention to the proper method of pruning an individual branch as well as to the process of selective thinning. When pruning a branch, make a cut beyond the branch-bark ridge, the swollen area at the branch base. It is a strong protective zone that will prevent decay from entering the tree after the cut. Thinning is the selective removal of branches from the shrub base, which keeps the crown open. This practice maximizes light penetration which keeps your shrub fully leafed out and healthy. The natural growth habit will be maintained while avoiding overstimulation of growth.

The main difference between decorating with greens outside versus inside is that when working outside, placing the greens in water is not an option in areas where temperatures fall below freezing. Generally, using fresh cut greens in the cooler outdoor environment ensures you of at least a month or two of enjoyment from your hard work. Let's explore the many options for the modern gardener to join in the fun of outdoor decorating.

Balsam (Abies balsamea)

Balsam (*Abies balsamea*) is by far the most widely used and least expensive

Balsam is a soft, flat-needled, densely sheared evergreen.

holiday green available. Balsam is a soft, flat-needled, densely sheared evergreen. Whether you have a few trees growing in the backyard that can be trimmed, or whether you purchase pre-cut bundles from your local garden center, balsam can form the bulk of your greens for pots or window boxes, if only because of its low cost. You will need a pair of

sharp pruning shears to cut your branches into different lengths—long, medium, and short. Generally pieces of 8, 12, and 18 to 24 inches long work best. This will allow you to layer your containers, giving interest and dimension to the final product.

White Pine (Pinus strobus)

White pine (*Pinus strobus*), since it tends to be plentiful and therefore also inexpensive, is used extensively for holiday decorating out of doors. A long-needled evergreen, white pine is

*White pine (*Pinus strobus*), since it tends to be plentiful and therefore also inexpensive, is used extensively for holiday decorating out of doors.*

a favorite for use as roping and in containers. Bundles of white pine are readily available at most nurseries, or can be clipped from trees already thriving in your yard. If your planter is not in direct sunlight and the weather remains cool (less than 40 degrees) white pine will last outside for several months.

White Cedar (Thuja occidentalis)

White cedar (*Thuja occidentalis*) is another green that is fairly plentiful and relatively inexpensive. A rather long-needled evergreen with stiff branches but long, flowing needles, white cedar adds majesty and elegance to your display. The color contrasts very well with the darker evergreens such as balsam or Fraser fir, creating interest and texture. In southern regions an equal substitute would be *Thuja orientalis*, or oriental arborvitae as it is commonly called.

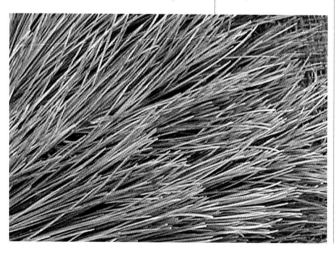

It is much more heat tolerant and thus holds its color better than other varieties, which helps where the holiday season routinely sees temperatures in the sixties. It will handle both warm and cold seasons, lasting well past Christmas. To expect two months or more is not unreasonable.

Juniper (Juniperus)

Juniper (*Juniperus*) is an excellent evergreen because of its vast color range and relative abundance. The juniper's ability to withstand drought and wind give it incredible needle retention when cut, adding to the longevity of your display. The color choices, ranging from blue to turquoise to greenish-yellow, afford the opportunity to get really creative. This is a green that will immediately draw your eye and should be incorporated in any outdoor display. Juniper is not too susceptible to sunburn, and as long as the tempera-

Boxwood (Buxus) *is an interesting evergreen, having woody stems with small ovate leaves.*

tures remain cool it should last for several months.

Boxwood (Buxus spp.)

Boxwood (*Buxus*) is an interesting evergreen, having woody stems with small ovate leaves. Used for centuries as a hedge, its petite, closely spaced leaves have accented arrangements from the palaces of kings, to the simple tables of peasants. If you plan to use boxwood outside, make sure of the variety. Many boxwoods are not cold hardy in northern climates, hence your beautiful outside planter, or roping incorporating boxwood, will look quite hideous in the morning following a below 32 degree night. The variety best suited for outdoor use is one native to your area. In the Northeast *Buxus v. koreana* (Korean boxwood) is highly cold tolerant, and the many hybrids offer a wide range of leaf size and color. *Buxus v. sempervirens* (common boxwood) is another cold-hardy species with countless varieties to choose from. The point is that if you plan to use boxwood outside, ask if what you are buying is native to the area; specifically, does your nursery sell this variety as a live shrub for outdoor planting? This will ensure you will not suffer the disappointment of brown "greens" in your beautiful pots.

Holly (Ilex)

Ilex, or holly, is another evergreen that adds a unique look to any outside display. Again, it is critical to determine if the holly you are buying will withstand the rigors of cold winter nights. As we discussed above with the boxwoods, make sure you ask your garden store professional whether the variety you are buying is cold hardy for your zone. The simplest way to obtain some is to cut sprigs from the holly bushes you may have had the foresight to plant in your yard a few years

When cutting holly, use the technique of selective "thinning," which is the removal of alternating branches from your shrub, which allows light to penetrate the interior, thus promoting renewed plant growth.

ago. Use the technique of selective "thinning," which is the removal of alternating branches from your shrub, which allows light to penetrate the interior, thus promoting renewed plant growth. *Ilex x merserveae* hybrids are the preferred species for northern climates. Their color ranges from blue to lustrous dark green, and the distinctive leathery serrated leaves will draw the eye of your Christmas visitors to any outside use of this plant. Some new hybridization has even led to variegated offerings within the series.

ROPING and GARLANDS
Making Your Own Garland

Roping is made by taking branches of evergreens, layering them vertically, and tying or wiring them to a center string. You can do this yourself but it can be very time consuming and tough on your fingers. If you want to give it a try, first decide what length you need. Use a strong but pliable wire and lay it out on a bench or table. Lay pieces of your preferred green, each about 10 to 12 inches long, on top of the wire, overlapping each piece as you move along the wire. Every 4 to 6 inches you will need to wire the branches to the central wire strand. This can also be done with a strong twine, preferably green to match your roping. You may have to tie in some additional

Roping is made by taking branches of evergreens, layering them vertically, and tying or wiring them to a center string.

wires to secure the roping so that the greens withstand any windy conditions they may encounter. Carefully wrap the wires tightly around the branches about every 5 to 6 inches. Twist the ends of each wire together and tuck it into the greens so it is not noticeable. Once you have completed the desired length, turn the rope over and begin the process again on the back side. When you have reached the end you will have a nice thick strand of homemade roping that you will be proud to display. For most of us this is a very time consuming process that will most likely only be undertaken once.

Purchasing Roping and Garland

Commercially produced rolls or coils of roping are readily available at the holidays and after reading about making roping yourself this may be the preferred route if you are looking to save some time and energy. The most common types of roping are white pine, cedar, boxwood, princess pine, and less often, balsam. White pine, as mentioned earlier, is relatively inexpensive and therefore the most commonly used. It will brown and dry easily, however, if exposed to full sun or very warm temperatures. There also seems to be great varia-

The most common types of roping are white pine, cedar, boxwood, princess pine, and less often, balsam.

tion in the quality or "grades" of white pine roping available. The old adage, "if it seems cheap, it probably is" applies, so shop carefully. We prefer using either cedar or a cedar/Douglas fir mix. It usually costs three times as much per yard as white pine, but it is very thick and luscious, well worth the extra dollars.

Another tip to remember is that most garland or roping material has

been cut and strung well in advance of the holidays. To extend its freshness, soak it in a tub or basin of warm water for at least an hour, and then let the roping drain. Towel dry before stringing it either outdoors or indoors. This, and periodic misting (two to three times per week), will greatly extend its decorative life span.

Decorating with Roping and Garland

Roping or garland is one of the main uses of greens for outside decorating, but works well and looks great indoors as well. Most roping used outdoors is hung on fences or used to frame a door. There are several steps to successfully use roping around the house. First measure as accurately as possible the length of roping you need. It is easier to work with a single piece than to have to piece shorter ones together later. If you have a straight run it is easy—just run a tape

To keep roping fresh, soak it in a tub or basin of water for at least an hour.

Below, a nicely draped garland.

measure along its length and get your reading in feet. Most roping is sold by the yard so remember that a yard equals three feet. If you plan to circle a lamppost or droop the roping along a fence, figure that you will need approximately one-third more than the length you have measured.

Now you are ready to hang your roping. Start with the end of your piece and hold it against the rail or doorframe. If you are attaching it to wood you can use a good, heavy-duty staple gun with ⅜- or ½-inch staples. Make sure you put the staple through the branches to firmly secure the roping. You can also use plastic or wire ties which are especially useful on railings or posts. Hold the roping firmly and pull the tie closed until snug. Trim off any excess so the tie blends into the roping. Finishing touches like a bright red bow or pinecones will make your home truly inviting for the holidays.

WREATHS

Evergreens have been used for thousands of years to decorate homes during the holidays. Evergreens are symbols of life, precisely because they remain green throughout the winter. Legend has it that evergreens held magical powers, and homes were decorated with them to bring good luck in the coming year.

Wreaths come in all kinds and varieties. They can be homemade, handcrafted, or made by machine. If you consider all the types of mixed green wreaths, the possibilities are limitless.

Balsam

Balsam is the most popular wreath material for the eastern half of the US. They are primarily produced in Maine and Canada, and are the most fragrant wreath of all. The aroma of balsam is the quintessential

Legend has it that evergreens held magical powers, and homes were decorated with them to bring good luck in the coming year.

Christmas fragrance. Balsam wreaths and greens are some of the least expensive available, adding to their popularity. The downside to balsam is its lack of longevity. If it is cold where you live the balsam will last longer hung outside on your door (barring direct sun on it) than some-

Balsam is the most popular wreath material for the eastern half of the US.

ture loss. Misting your wreath two to three times per week would also help for those warmer periods.

Juniper

Juniper is a great choice when you prefer not to use materials of a deep green color. The foliage and berries both have a blue cast. It makes an interesting show but also allows the wreath decorations to be the center of attention. Juniper wreaths are slightly more expensive than balsam; however, an advantage is that unlike balsam, juniper still looks "fresh" even when becoming dry.

Fraser Fir

Fraser firs have been increasing in popularity recently, primarily because of their longevity. Most people have seen them offered as Christmas trees, but they are also available as cut greens and wreaths. A Fraser wreath has a look reminiscent of balsam,

where where it is warm. Balsam dries out fairly quickly if it is above 40 degrees, so take this into consideration when deciding to use it. If you know your wreath will be in these warm conditions you may want to apply a coating of Wilt-Pruf, an anti-transpirant which will retard mois-

without the fragrance and with a blue color on the underside of the needle. They also last twice as long as balsam, so if you leave your wreath up for months, this is the one to find! You can mist Fraser fir but like juniper, it looks as good as new even when dry, so the effort may not be necessary.

White Pine

Many people like the soft look of a white pine wreath and its vibrant green color. The only downside to using white pine as a wreath is that

Many people like the soft look of a white pine wreath and its vibrant green color.

its long needles make it harder to decorate because they tend to bend and not hold ornaments quite so well. It also doesn't have as full an appearance as most of the other wreaths.

Noble Fir/ Mixed Greens

Noble fir with other mixed greens is a common choice for wreaths for the western US. The abundance of this type of tree in the western states makes the economics favorable for local wreath making for the Pacific states markets. Noble fir is durable, beautiful, and very symmetrical. It is also an excellent base for the many kinds of mixed-green wreaths that are produced. Almost any green can be added to a noble fir wreath. It is very easy to add greens and decorations to noble fir because its branches are so stiff. This allows them to be wired firmly in place.

The color of noble fir, a rich dark green with striking brown stems, also enhances the color of other evergreens, making the contrast quite spectacular. Noble fir seems to possess the same ability as Fraser fir to remain in near-perfect condition even when allowed to become quite dry. It certainly deserves its name as a "noble" fir.

Making Your Own

Many people prefer to make their own wreaths for their doors. Once you have made one, it's a project you can do every year. It does require some effort and time, so be prepared to spend at least two hours in making and decorating the wreath.

You begin with a wreath frame, which you can

Many people prefer to make their own wreaths for their doors.

find at a craft store or large garden centers. Generally there are "teeth" attached to the circular frame. You can lay your greens, that have already been cut to short lengths (approximately 8 inches) inside the teeth, overlapping and going around the frame.

When you have determined that a section is full enough, bend the teeth down into the greens trying to

1. Cut your greens in pieces approximately 8" long.

2. Place the branches inside the teeth, overlapping until the section looks full.

3. Bend the teeth down to hold the greens in place.

4. Trim off any unsightly ends.

5. Cover any bare spots with additional smaller pieces.

hide them in the foliage. It takes some practice, but this method is easier than just using a circular frame where you have to wire the greens to the frame. If you can't find a frame with teeth, other styles are available. When using wire, start by securing the branches at the base of the stem and then again in the middle. For the next piece, place it under the tip of the last branch so you don't see the stem end. Work your way around the frame until you are back where you started. You can always add small pieces anywhere there is a bare spot or to make it fuller and fluffier. If you are using a frame with teeth you may want to have some wire on hand to use as well when adding smaller pieces to fill sparse places.

We recommend using firs such as balsam or Fraser for a fuller, wider wreath. Actually any kind of greens are appropriate; it's a matter of personal preference. You may have a

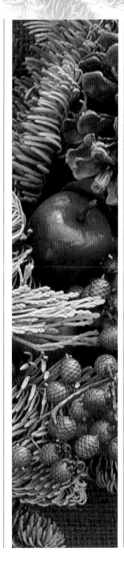

tree or shrub that could stand a little pruning, and you can use the scraps for creating a wreath or swag. Often the bottom branches from your Christmas tree can be used for this purpose. Short on time? Another option is to purchase a wreath that is undecorated, and then decorate it yourself. It is not hard to do, and shouldn't take more than an hour if you have all your supplies.

Trimming

Trimming your wreath is the next step. After you have made or purchased your wreath, decide what kinds of decorations you want and what color ribbon or bow you would like to use. An important consideration about the decorations and ribbons is whether or not they are weatherproof or weather resistant. If your creation will be subjected to harsh elements such as rain, snow, or sleet, choose your decorations wisely.

Now you're ready to put your own decorations on your wreath. You'll need a glue gun, or glue pot, and some florist wire (all available at craft stores). The glue is not essential but florist wire alone is time consuming and will most likely make your project take much longer.

Some items like pine cones can be wired together in bunches of three, then you use the excess wire that is left to attach them to the wreath all at once. Although this can be time consuming, if the wreath is hung in a windy area the trimmings will tend to be more secure with this method. Using the glue gun as well speeds up this process, and once you are used to working with glue you'll prefer it. One trick we have learned about glue is that you need to press hard and use enough so that it gets well down into the greens so they will stay on and look better.

Attach the florist wire to a bow and wire it onto your wreath. Bows can be placed at the top or bottom of a wreath.

If you like a natural look, simply use pinecones, either singly or in threes (odd numbers look best), some red berries, and your bow. Wow, that was easy! If you prefer the fancier styles, use wired ribbon (which is easier to use to make a bow) and glass balls (which are pre-wired), or whatever suits your fancy; that's the fun part, it's your wreath, so anything goes!!!

Decorating can be simple, like draping garland around a doorway, or elegant, such as adorning an old light fixture with greens and ornaments.

A *pinecone and ornament wreath, a simple door wreath, or an overstuffed bowl of pinecones can all make your home alive with fun for the holidays.*

CHOOSING YOUR TREE

As with the poinsettia, the Christmas tree has a long and storied past where fact and fantasy interweave so as to be practically indistinguishable. The earliest recorded tales of decorated trees being used in celebration can be traced to the ancient Romans. During the winter festival of Saturnalia, honoring Saturn, the god of agriculture, Romans would hang small pieces of metal from the branches of trees in hopes of pleasing the provider of their sustenance. During the Middle Ages, on December 24, apples were strung on an evergreen which was then dubbed the Paradise tree.

Using an evergreen clearly seems to have originated in the forests of Europe. Markets in Alsace record their sale as early as 1531. This

As with the poinsettia, the Christmas tree has a long and storied past where fact and fantasy interweave.

would lend some credence to the mythical story of Martin Luther being the first to decorate a tree, inspired by his walk in the forest surrounded by evergreens adorned with the sparkling stars above. Fact or fiction, we'll never really know. Nonetheless, the oldest record of a decorated Christmas tree comes from a 1605 diary found in Strasbourg, France (which was part of Germany at the time). The tree was decorated with apples, candles, and paper roses. In America, the custom seems to have been brought by Hessian soldiers during the War for Independence and embraced mostly by early German settlers. Charles Minnegrode brought the custom of decorating evergreens to Williamsburg, Virginia in 1842, but it didn't hit the East Coast until an enterprising young man named Mark Carr brought trees from the Catskills to the streets of New York City in 1851. As with most

Shape and color are both important aspects in choosing a tree.

anything else in our country, once New York takes a fancy to it the phenomenon is off and running. Today the commercial production of Christmas trees for the US is a multi-billion dollar business.

The type of tree your family considers the "perfect" Christmas tree is probably different from that of your neighbors. Much depends on what part of the country you are from, or more importantly, what your family had when you were growing up. For most of us nothing can beat the fragrance or feel of a fresh-cut tree. As I describe the various types and where you are likely to find them, sit back, sip your hot chocolate, and let visions of Christmas flood your mind.

Balsam

Abies (the firs) is the genus of two of the five most popular Christmas trees. Balsam fir (*Abies balsamea*) are best suited to conditions in colder climates and hence have, until recent years, been the dominant species for cut-tree use in the Northeast. The balsam's relatively stiff branches and generally conical growth habit make it the poster child for Christmas trees everywhere. When you add in its distinctive evergreen fragrance, you have a sure winner. Its fairly acceptable growth rate of about 1½ feet a year, producing a salable tree in five to seven years, also makes it fairly economical, considering most are grown in the colder reaches of the Northeast and Canada before being trucked to more populated metropolitan areas, where they sell for between $20 and $50. Since they do prefer moist, well-drained soil for best growth, and the recent hot, dry seasons in the Northeast have decreased the balsam's expected shelf life, two to three weeks is the most balsam should be kept in your home for maximum safety.

The balsam's relatively stiff branches and generally conical growth habit make it the poster child for Christmas trees everywhere.

With a similar appearance to the balsam, but with a distinct bluish tinge to its needles, the Fraser has won the hearts and minds of families everywhere.

Fraser Fir

The Fraser fir (*Abies fraseri*) is the rising star of Christmas trees. In 1993, 2500 North Carolina tree growers planted over 30,000 acres, with each acre producing 2700 trees—quite a site! With a similar appearance to the balsam, but with a distinct bluish tinge to its needles, the Fraser has won the hearts and minds of families everywhere. What has really been the Fraser's claim to fame, however, is its ability to retain its needles for longer than its nearest competitor—the balsam. The first year I put one in my store for the holidays it got quickly forgotten during the hustle and bustle of the season. In late February when we reopened the Fraser still looked like we just put it up. Although dry, it held its needles even when we jostled and shook the tree during its removal. While I certainly do not recommend leaving your Fraser up beyond three weeks, there is comfort in knowing you could, and that it is the tree of choice for warmer, drier houses, like those with wood stoves or forced air. This staying power will cost you however; Frasers generally run $10 to $15 more than a comparably sized alternative.

Other Abies

Other *Abies* contenders include noble fir (*Abies procera*) and white or concolor fir (*Abies concolor*). Noble firs are native to the mountainous regions of the western US where they

Noble firs are native to the mountainous regions of the western US where they thrive on the cool, moist, acidic soil conditions.

thrive on the cool, moist, acidic soil conditions. Its short needles that point vertically upward give it a noble appearance. Concolor fir has a silvery appearance to its branches combined with a bluish-green tint to its needles, again creating a distinctive look. Native to southern California, Mexico, and the southwestern US, this is a variety with limited mass appeal due to commercial growing limitations, but it has made some inroads in the eastern US, showing up more and more every year. Both the noble and concolor firs are better candidates for the house with a large atrium or cathedral ceiling, since they are best appreciated on a larger, more majestic scale as reflects their native habitat.

Douglas firs have a needle somewhat longer than balsam or Fraser firs, and have a much softer feel to the touch. This softer feel can work against it as a Christmas tree since the heavy ornaments can cause the branches to sag under their weight.

Douglas Fir

Pseudotsuga menziesii, or Douglas fir, is the third offering in our top five favorite Christmas trees. Native to the Rocky Mountains and the Northwest, it has migrated eastward, mostly into Pennsylvania, for commercial cut-tree production. This has an advantage during times of regional drought. Ask your tree seller if the "Dougs" are West- or East-Coast grown if you know one or the other of the areas has experienced recent dry spells. Douglas firs have a needle somewhat longer than balsam or Fraser firs, and have a much softer feel to the touch. This softer feel can work against it as a Christmas tree since the heavy ornaments can cause the branches to sag under their weight. The unique "citrus" smell and yellowish-green color will give you pause as you wander the tree lot in search of the perfect tree.

Scotch Pine

The fourth heavy hitter in the world of Christmas trees is *Pinus sylvestris*, or Scotch pine. Once the most widespread species throughout Europe, it made its way to the US as a good source of timber. It was also once the most widely used for Christmas trees. Its ready availability, long needles, and stately appearance made it the family favorite pretty much nationwide. It has fallen out of favor in the last ten years for various reasons, not the least of which is the rise of Fraser fir. Scotch pine has also suffered somewhat from the proliferation of breeding efforts, which led to tremendous variability in needle length, hardiness, growth habit, and adaptability. Diseases such as pine wilt fungus and diplodia, as well as its inability to withstand heat or drought have combined to marginalize the Scotch pine in the cut-tree market today.

Above, you can see the long needles of a scotch pine.
Below, the beautiful and abundant Eastern white pine.

Eastern White Pine

While there are other pines worth mentioning as possible choices for cut tree use, our personal favorite is *Pinus strobus* or Eastern white pine. Introduced to the US in 1705 it has adapted well, seeding itself so easily it got the nickname "Old Field Pine." What has limited its popularity as a Christmas tree is the great variation in color, plus the fact that it can look rather sparse if it has not been sheared properly from a young age. I have even seen white pines on tree lots that have been dyed dark green to make them more appealing. Check the trunk for telltale dye run marks if this is a concern for you. White pines will not hold their needles for long, and should not be inside for more than seven to ten days. For some, they evoke a Christmas from a much simpler time, when it was the rule rather than the exception to venture into the field and cut down one of the numerous field-grown pines. For that reason alone, white pines deserve some serious consideration and, in addition, they usually run about a third less in cost than most other trees.

Now that we have covered the top five we should at least discuss a few other choices for those adventurous souls who like to fly in the face of convention. Here we venture into the world of *Picea* or spruce. The spruce family is valued primarily for its use in the pulp and paper industries, and for its resinous bark, which is the major component of many varnishes. However, it is their pyramidal and conical shape with a dense growth habit that can make them candidates for the place of honor in your Christmas decorating plans. While there are many varieties, here we will discuss only the two likeliest candidates for Christmas.

While there are other pines worth mentioning as possible choices for cut tree use, our personal favorite is Pinus strobus *or Eastern white pine. Introduced to the US in 1705 it has adapted well, seeding itself so easily it got the nickname "Old Field Pine."*

Picea abies, or Norway spruce, is still the favorite in Britain as well as other regions of northern Europe. With its short, densely packed needles, and lush dark green color, the Norway spruce will certainly cause your holiday visitors to take notice.

Norway Spruce

Picea abies, or Norway spruce, is still the favorite in Britain as well as other regions of northern Europe. With its short, densely packed needles, and lush dark green color, the Norway spruce will certainly cause your holiday visitors to take notice. Its dark bark adds a nice contrast. A stately tree, it certainly warrants a consideration if you can find one on a commercial lot. You might have better luck in a cut-your-own operation, or in your own backyard. After all, cutting a tree down in your own landscape will get you back to the garden center in the spring!

Colorado Spruce

Picea pungens, or Colorado spruce, is another of the species that should be thought of at Christmas time. At first pause you might say, "Why, aren't they awful expensive?" Well, the answer is yes, and they are slow growing, however some species' brilliant blue color can be well worth the expense. Add in the fact that most people are so struck by the color when planting them as a live tree, they oftentimes place them in the wrong part of the landscape. If planted in the front yard they will draw anyone's eye from your other plantings, quite possibly from your house itself. It might just be the time to bundle up the family, trek out to big blue and saw away. Since it is a spruce, its stately growth habit and strong branches will handle all your ornaments as well as produce a stunning visual effect.

Picking a Fresh Tree

Now that you have all the information you need to decide on the type of tree you want, you need to know a few things about completing your selection, getting it home, and giving it proper care to ensure it lasts well beyond December 25.

Picea pungens, *or Colorado spruce, is another of the species that should be thought of at Christmas time.*

As you wander through the tree lot do not just consider the shape of the tree alone. Grasp the end of a branch firmly between your thumb and index finger and pull toward you. If no needles pull off in your hand, the tree is fresh. If four or more needles come off, look for another tree.

There are several surefire methods for picking the perfect Christmas tree. As you wander through the tree lot do not just consider the shape of the tree alone. Grasp the end of a branch firmly between your thumb and index finger and pull toward you. If no needles pull off in your hand, the tree is fresh. If four or more needles come off, look for another tree. You should also bend the end of a branch sharply back onto itself. Look for the branch end to snap back swiftly, not remain in a folded position. Look the tree over and do not be afraid to ask the salesperson to hold the tree and spin it around for you to see it from all sides. If there are some brown needles deep inside, especially near the bottom, it doesn't mean that it is necessarily a bad tree. On tree farms that heavily shear their trees, some interior needle loss is to be expected. Just make sure you perform the two tests above to ensure the tree is fresh.

Caring for Your Tree

Always carry a tarp or blanket for tree wrapping and protection when transporting your cut tree in a pickup truck, or when tying it to the car roof. Prolonged exposure to a cold wind (a car traveling at 40 miles an hour will generate such a wind) will substantially dry out any tree, decreasing its freshness and lasting power. You should spread the tarp or sheet out on the ground, laying the

Always carry a tarp or blanket for tree wrapping and protection when transporting your cut tree in a pickup truck, or when tying it to the car roof.

tree on top. Tightly wrap it around the tree and secure the bundle with bungee cords or strong twine. Now your tree is ready to be carried to the roof of the car or bed of the pickup truck. Make sure the tarp covers the fresh cut on the butt, as wind can cause the cut to heal over quickly, thus reducing the ability of your tree to drink water when you get it in the stand. Remember, getting your tree to drink water is critical to maximizing the amount of time you can safely keep it indoors.

After bringing your cut tree home, you need to drag out your Christmas tree stand. Everyone at one time or other has tried to use one of those old rickety, three-legged stands with the turnbuckle screws. You've probably also had a tree or two topple over when using one as well. Having the right stand seems like a no-brainer, but you'd be surprised. Here are a few helpful hints

designed to convince you to throw that old stand out and make your holiday easier with the right stand. First, make sure you choose a stand that is large enough for the size tree you want. There is nothing worse than having to try and wittle down the trunk of an 8 foot tree to get it to fit a small stand. Next, choose a stand with a solid, flat base that is large enough to create stability; 12 to 18 inches square works well. Now, make sure the trunk opening is large enough to accommodate the size of the tree you generally buy. Your stand should have four, not three, securing screws as this provides a more stable anchoring mechanism. Lastly, the water reservoir must be large enough to provide a good supply of water for your tree. This will be critical for long-term tree care. Some garden stores and nurseries use bottom-drilled trees and spike stands. These can be good because the tree

Before placing your tree in the stand it needs a fresh cut off of the bottom of the trunk.

sits firmly on and anchors to the spike on the stand; however, make sure the tree seller makes a fresh base cut, redrills the tree, and makes a straight hole. Otherwise you'll be looking at a crooked tree all season.

Now that you've found the correct stand, let's get your tree ready to move indoors. Before placing your tree in the stand it needs a fresh cut off of the bottom of the trunk. Ideally when you get the tree home you

Put the tree in a bucket of warm water while waiting to set it up in its final display location.

should immediately cut at least ½ inch from the base with a sharp saw and put the tree in a bucket of warm water while waiting to set it up in its final display location. You can have the tree seller cut the tree for you but if you do, it must get into water in less than one hour. Either way a fresh cut must be made, because it will remove the gum callus on the bottom of the tree and enable more efficient water uptake, extending

freshness. People often ask if they should use a preservative in the water. It doesn't hurt and it certainly makes some sense. Commercial preservatives have been formulated to enhance fluid uptake in trees and plants, so they should be of benefit to your Christmas tree. An aspirin in the water will also aid in liquid uptake. A clear sugar soda has been known to keep a cut evergreen vibrant for a longer period of time, however the evidence is mostly anecdotal.

Experiment, but whatever you do, do *not* let the water level in your stand fall below the cut of the tree. Remember that it only takes an hour or less for the butt to heal over. An especially critical time is just after you have put the tree in the stand. Once inside, the tree warms up and awakens from its slumber, very thirsty indeed. It is not uncommon to leave a full stand when you go to bed that first night, only to rise in the morning to no water. Try leaving the tree in an unheated garage in a bucket of water for a day or so. This will give it adequate time to gulp large quantities of water prior, to mounting in your stand, and should help get it through the night until you can fill the stand again. If your stand should run dry, you should fill it immediately. As a precaution, you can also drill holes in the sides of the trunk below the water line. This will help open up new avenues for water uptake.

Live Trees

At some point in their lives, many people will decide that it would be a wonderful idea to use a live tree at Christmas. This is always a hit-or-miss proposition. Once you break a tree's dormancy by bringing it indoors, then place it outdoors again in possibly harsh conditions, you run the risk of damaging the tree beyond recovery. You can improve your odds

Keep the soil you remove from the hole in a wheelbarrow . . .

by following a few commonsense gardening techniques.

If you're planning to purchase a live Christmas tree in a northern climate, dig the hole for its planting well before the holidays, when the ground is still unfrozen. There is nothing worse than trudging out to the yard in January, only to find the ground dents your shovel! Keep the soil you remove from the hole in a wheelbarrow and cover it or store it in the shed or garage where it won't freeze. This will improve the odds of a successful transplant. When moving an evergreen into the house as a living Christmas tree, do so in stages. An abrupt transition from subfreezing outdoor temperatures to 70-plus degrees will cause plant shock. Instead, move the tree into an environment with a more moderate temperature, such as a garage, for a few days to lessen the shock. You should do the same on the way out of the house when it's time to plant the tree into the yard. We recommend that you keep a live tree indoors no longer than seven to ten days. Anything beyond this and you run the risk of breaking the tree's dormancy. Almost any potted or burlapped live evergreen is suitable for use as a living Christmas tree. Generally you will find Norway or blue spruces as well as Douglas firs in most garden shops at Christmas. The tree of choice ultimately

. . . and cover it or store it in the shed or garage where it won't freeze.

depends on how much money you want to risk. Since the survival rate for transplanting evergreens in January can be anywhere from 50 to 70 percent, the more you spend on the tree the more you stand to lose if it doesn't make it. A 5 to 6 foot live tree can run anywhere from $75 to $150, so the decision is one not to be taken too lightly. Follow our rule above regarding a short indoor stay and your odds will improve greatly.

FUN HOLIDAY PROJECTS

Window Boxes

Window boxes are a fun holiday endeavor. Ever wondered what to do with your window boxes and garden containers for the winter? Well, if you live in the colder parts of the US and your flowers are all gone at the start of the Christmas season, don't despair. It's very easy to dress up those window boxes or large pots. The first step is to have either soil or Styrofoam in your container. You'll need something to anchor your greens in.

Using balsam, Douglas, Fraser, or whatever green you like as your background, cover your container or box with the greens, using pieces that are at least 12 to 18 inches long. You want it to be dense enough so that you can't see the inside of the container. When you are finished "greening" the pot, you can then decorate with ribbons, bows, white birch branches, pine cones, other types of greens, etc. These containers will last all winter. It is great to see evergreens during the long days of winter, so don't put away your pretty pots or window boxes just because it's getting cold!

Swags are easier to make than wreaths, and for some evoke memories of a simpler time.

Swag

Another fun project is making a swag. Swags are even easier to make than wreaths since they don't require a frame. Swags are triangular in shape, so keep that in mind when choosing the back piece. Often when you purchase greens cut in bunches you will find a good piece for your back or base. The length of this piece will depend on how big you want your swag to be. For a standard 3 foot by 7 foot door, your back piece should be 12 to 18 inches. Lay it on the worktable. Now choose your next three or four pieces and lay them on top. Each piece should be a little smaller than the last. Noble fir makes a good background piece, and incense cedar and juniper make nice accent pieces for the top two layers. Take florist wire (any thin wire will do) and wrap very tightly around the top (underneath where the pine cones are in the photo) where your main branches meet. Now you're ready to add your personal touches. Pinecones, ribbon, berries, statice, and baby's breath are great additions. Wire these to branches of the swag with the florist wire. Include a small loop of wire at the top of the back of the swag for hanging. Now it's ready to be hung on your door, or anywhere you need some greenery.

Kissing balls are easy to make and have been increasing in popularity.

Kissing Balls

Kissing balls have been increasing in popularity in recent years. They originated as mistletoe balls wrapped with ribbon, used in place of hanging sprigs of mistletoe. Now kissing balls are made with fresh or artificial greens and decorated. The easiest method is to find a pre-made ball, which you can then decorate. You can purchase them at florists or garden centers, or find artificial ones at craft stores. You can even use a spherical ball of Styrofoam which is also found in craft shops. This is much more time consuming and we don't recommend it for the busy novice, but if you must, here's how. Cut a piece of ribbon 12 to 18 inches and secure it to the top of the ball with a small finishing nail. Now cut 4 to 5 inch pieces of fresh greens (we prefer balsam—it's cheap and readily available) and stick the thicker stem portion into the Styrofoam. Continue until the entire ball is covered in greens and you can not see any more Styrofoam. Now for the fun part! These are decorated very similarly to wreaths or swags. You can use pinecones, as we have, glass balls, statice, or baby's breath, and ribbons. The simplest method of attaching your trimmings is to wire the decorations to a wooden pick and then stick the pick into the Styrofoam center. Smaller items could be glued on with a glue gun, if you have one. Kissing balls can be hung in a variety of places around the home, such as outside your door; instead of a wreath on your hanging basket bracket, or on a lamppost; or you can use them inside your home instead of mistletoe. If you choose that option, to prolong its freshness you should mist it with water every few days.

Kissing balls are decorated very similarly to wreaths or swags. You can use pinecones, as we have, glass balls, statice, or baby's breath, and ribbons.

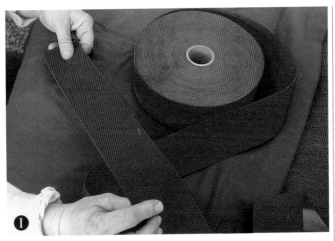

Above, about 12" of ribbon should be left at the start, to become a tail later. Below, pinching the ribbon to create the first loop.

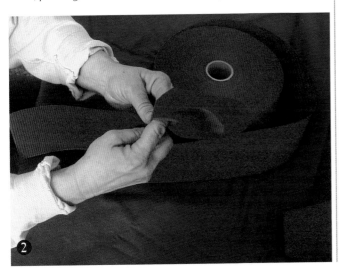

Bows

Making your own bows is another fun holiday project. We can't tell you how many people have said they could never make a bow. Well, we are here to tell you that we were not born knowing how to make a bow. Purchase the ribbon you like and we'll take you step by step. Wired ribbon is more expensive, but offers a better finished appearance and is much easier to work with. Make sure you buy enough so that you can practice with some extra that you'll throw away. You'll need approximately 2 ½ to 3 yards to make a bow large enough for a wreath that would go on a door. Larger wreaths require more ribbon. Take about 12 inches and leave that piece hanging, it will become one of the tails. In one hand, using your thumb, first, and second fingers, pinch the ribbon together and make your first loop. You are going to repeat this step for every loop you

Left, continue to make loops on both sides of the bow. Don't forget to keep the ribbon pinched very tight.

Right, when you have completed all six loops you can cut the ribbon. Now, begin to wire your bow together by running the wire through the loop and over exactly where the ribbon is being pinched.

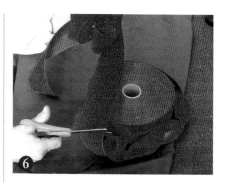

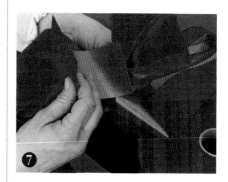

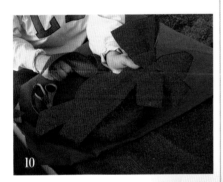

Step 9, left, pull the wire very tight and twist until it cannot come undone.

Fluff out the loops by pulling and separating them, Step 10.

loops are even on both sides (you want them to be the same size). You can measure your loops to see if they are even, by holding them side by side. (See picture 4.) The last two loops, which will form the front of the bow, can be slightly smaller than the others if you like. Make six loops, three on each side, and if you have done it correctly you can cut the ribbon (it's going to become the other tail, so don't cut it too short). Now you have the completed bow in your hand. If you would like to add a little fancy touch, with your free hand, cut a five to six inch piece and fold it over as shown to make a final extra loop and a more professional looking bow. Take a piece of florist wire and run it between your first and second fingers and then through the loop and over where the ribbon is pinched between your fingers. (The wire should be in the exact middle of the bow—see picture 8.) Pull very tight, and twist the wire,

make, doing one loop on one side and then one on the opposite side. Make sure you are holding the ribbon very tightly where it's pinched together. This is the most important part of making a bow; if the ribbon isn't held tightly enough the bow will be floppy and won't look right. Make sure your

again very tight. If it's tight enough, you will be able to fluff out the loops by pulling and separating them, then straighten any loop that needs it without ruining the bow. Don't give up, try making several and you'll get it—this just takes practice! Hint—smaller-width ribbons look better with more loops, so try using four to five loops on each side, and don't skimp. Large

wreaths need lots of ribbon; it is a good idea to use an even wider ribbon for them and to make the bow in stages, because it is too hard to hold all that ribbon all at once.

Candle Ring

It is not hard to make your own candle ring or centerpiece adorned with berries and cones. This is similar to making a kissing ball. Obtain a Styrofoam or floral foam ring from your garden shop or craft store. Cut 3 to 4 inches lengths of fresh greens such as balsam or noble fir. Push them into the foam so that you cover the entire ring. Add sprigs of juniper or arborvitae for color contrast. Statice or baby's breath, also available from your garden shop, adds an extra level of interest. Small bows and a brightly colored candle finish this elegant addition to the holiday table.

One of the most fun parts of the holiday is decorating within your home. Nothing broadens your possibilities more than incorporating greens with your own decorations. This can be something as simple as laying branches on your mantle and placing Christmas ornaments in among them. You can place boughs in nooks and crannies highlighted with live plants or shiny balls.

Roping can be incorporated inside the home as well. Strung on banisters or draped around light fixtures it can create a very festive atmosphere. Hang a few ornaments or lights along the roping and you will impress any jaded holiday visitor!

Topiaries

Holiday topiaries are easy to make. In the late summer or early fall pick up a pot of rosemary from your local garden center or dig one from your garden. Choose a nice pot, something decorative is nice but I prefer the look of a plain clay pot. Now

One of the most fun parts of the holiday is decorating within your home.

place a topiary ring firmly into the pot. These rings are readily available in craft stores or your local nursery. They usually have a nice base with either a circular ring or prongs that wedge easily into your pot. This is why a ceramic or clay pot works best because these are solid, heavy bases that will anchor your ring and prevent your finished topiary from being top heavy. If you have trouble finding a topiary ring, take a metal coat hanger, and shape the triangular section into a round or spherical configuration. Then bend the hook part, so that it becomes perpendicular to the rest of the now-reformed coat hanger to create your base. Now place this into your pot and you're ready to continue.

Take the rosemary out of its container, make sure the roots are creamy white (which ensures that the plant is healthy) and place it into your new pot to one side of the topiary ring. Fill the pot with soil, being careful to not pack or push the soil too hard around the existing rosemary plant's soil ball. This could lead to soil compaction, which can reduce air space, resulting in diminished oxygen uptake by the roots. Wind the branches around the ring, securing them with green florist's tape. Make sure you don't twist them too tightly or you risk damaging the branch. If the ties are too tight, as the plant stems grow the tie can actually cut into the stem damaging the plant cell layers within. This will destroy the plant's ability to transport vital nutrients and water to all of its branches. Secure the tips at the top with twist-ties. Now trim the shoots into a nice shape. This is just like trimming a beard or a shrub in your yard. The idea is to give your topiary a rounded, finished look. You will need to trim as the topiary grows to maintain the shape you want. Save these trimmings; you can dry them

After picking a healthy plant and repotting it, be sure to secure the branches loose enough for your plant to have room to grow.

by laying them out on a tray for a day, or bundling a few together and hanging them above a window in your kitchen area. After three or four days you can place them in a tightly sealed jar for flavoring those hearty stews in the cold winter months ahead.

After your topiary has been neatly trimmed place it in the sunniest window you can find, preferably in the kitchen. This will make sure your topiary is readily available for not only its wonderful aroma but also for a quick snip and addition to the evening's meal. There, you did it; won't your friends be impressed?

Trim your topiary to maintain its shape and to give it a rounded, finished look.

HERB

ARP
ROSEMARY

Gingerbread House

The ultimate holiday project is a gingerbread house. The aroma of baking gingerbread brings back memories for many of us. While not plant related, it certainly adds a unique dimension to any home's holiday décor. More importantly, it is a wonderful way to gather friends and family together to work on a fun project that can be carried on throughout the season. We have made many gingerbread houses and people who see them often say they can't imagine doing it themselves. Remember, we had a first time too. On a wind swept hill in a snow-covered Maine farmhouse we learned the art of gingerbread houses from my uncle's wife, Judy. So now we are going to pass that knowledge on to you, too!

The ultimate holiday project is a gingerbread house. The aroma of baking gingerbread brings back memories for many of us.

Here are some first time guidelines to follow:

- Start with a small building or purchase a kit. (The kits are available at craft stores.)

- Go slowly; don't expect it to be finished in a hurry.

- Have your children or friends help.

- Enjoy the process!

First you'll want to find a pattern of a house you'd like to construct. The women's magazines always have several patterns in their holiday issues, usually associated with a contest. One important tip we have is that you should start early, especially if it is a large house. We usually begin in mid-November. Start with an easy boxy type of pattern that doesn't have many different rooflines. Have all your pattern pieces ready for your gingerbread dough. This recipe is one I have

Sugar, spice, and everything nice is what makes gingerbread houses look and taste so good.

used for years; it tastes good and is easy to work with.

Dough prep:

1 cup shortening

1 cup butter

about 8 cups flour

1 teaspoon each ground cinnamon, allspice, cloves, and ginger

2 heaping teaspoons baking powder

½ cup milk

2 cups molasses (1 jar)

1 pound brown sugar

Melt shortening and butter together. While melting, sift the spices with the 8 cups of flour, and then dissolve baking powder in milk. We use a heavy-duty mixer, but mixing and kneading by hand will work as well, though it tends to take longer and is tough on the wrists. Mix the molasses, sugar, and the melted butter mixture. Add the milk, and then stir in about 7 cups of the flour and spice mix. Add the remaining flour as needed to make malleable dough. The dough will be very heavy and thick. Shape your dough into a ball and wrap in wax paper or plastic wrap. Put it in the refrigerator for at least three to four hours, or preferably overnight. This dough will keep in the fridge (wrapped) for at least a week.

When you have decided to start, let the dough warm slightly before rolling out very thin, to about ⅟₁₆ inch. We roll our dough out on the

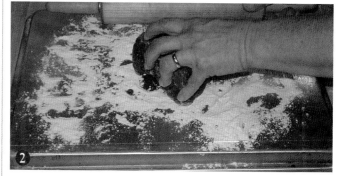

Simply mix, roll, trim, shape, and bake, and you are ready to start building your very own gingerbread house.

back of a well-floured cookie sheet. This saves transferring the cut pieces, which is not easy. We have also found that using a sleeve on the rolling pin makes this part much easier. You can find rolling pin sleeves in the baking section of your supermarket. You then cut out all your pieces using your patterns and bake at 325–350 degrees for about 10 minutes. We like to use slightly thicker dough for the supporting walls, and this adds a few more minutes to the baking time. You will know the dough is ready when it turns dark brown (not black) in color, and is firm. Watch the dough closely in the last few minutes of baking, because once it begins to turn dark brown it will burn very quickly. It is best to check it every 30 seconds during the last 2 minutes of cooking time. Store the gingerbread somewhere cool and dry, where it won't get broken. It is a good idea to bake an extra piece or two in case something breaks or you need a piece for an added decoration, or perhaps you forgot to bake two of some piece!

Meanwhile, you should have a strong piece of cardboard or plywood, covered with aluminum foil, to build your house on. This is critical, so when choosing between cardboard and wood, imagine how heavy the house will be and then decide which would be better. If you want to be able to move it around to display it, use plywood. You will be covering the aluminum foil with frosting so don't worry about messes; it will be one of the last things you'll frost.

Now for the fun part! Let's build your house. First you will need frosting, for your "glue." This is what holds the house together, and you use it for decorating also. We make it in small batches, because it dries out quickly and shouldn't be stored in the fridge if you can help it.

Here's the recipe:

1½ cups sifted confectioners' sugar

pinch salt

1 egg white

1 teaspoon lemon juice

Think about how much you want to get done at a time and make

items. If you do mix less frosting plan on mixing 2 to 3 minutes less, but just watch it carefully; the real measure is it should be light and fluffy. The longer you beat it, the better glue it makes—to a point. You have to get a feel for what light and fluffy is. Too much mixing and you may have trouble with the icing smoothly exiting the pastry bag. You may have to go through a few batches until you get the feel—but that's okay, it's actually a good experience that will give you confidence for fancier techniques later on. Now cover the bowl of icing with a damp cloth.

Next you will need a pastry tube, including the three to four tips that usually come with any pastry kit, also available in grocery stores. Fill the tube about ⅔ full and, using the pencil tip, you can pipe the frosting to be used as the glue for your construction. You can use a plastic sandwich bag with a hole in the corner if you don't

just enough; we usually triple this recipe. Beat all the ingredients with an electric mixer until light and fluffy. We have found that it takes about 6 to 8 minutes for a triple batch, made in a heavy duty dough mixer of at least 250 watts. A triple batch is the best amount if you are planning to work on more than trim

have a pastry bag, but we have found once you have made one gingerbread house, you'll want to do more, and it is so much easier with the bag and all the different tips.

Take your end wall and pipe frosting along the ground, and place a canned good item next to it to hold it up. Here is another opportunity for your kids or friends to help. Then take your second wall, the adjacent one to the first wall, and pipe frosting on the ground and up the seam. Place another can to hold that wall steady, and make sure you clean up any extra frosting that is on the walls right away—it hardens fairly quickly so wipe it off frequently. Don't worry so much about smaller globs that are on the ground; they will be easy to cover later when you are covering the rest of your foil. Let this frosting on the walls set and harden for a while. Finish the base of the house. It is a good idea to wait for twenty-four

Pipe frosting along the ground, and use a canned good for stability, in order to create your first wall. Once dry, pipe frosting on the ground and up the seam to attach your second wall.

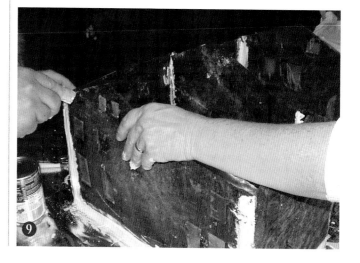

Above, continue piping frosting on the ground and up the seams for all of your walls. Below, attach the roof after your walls have had ample time to dry.

hours to put the roof on; this gives the frosting a chance to really harden. If your house is large you may want to put a supporting piece in the center for added support for the roof. The roof should be assembled one piece at a time once your walls are together, just as if you were building a real house. Once one side of the roof is attached and secured with a bead, or a thin line of icing at all points where it touches the walls, attach the second half. Run another bead of icing along the top of the ridge peak to secure the entire roof. It's best to let the whole house now sit overnight.

Now that your house is constructed its time to decorate! Decide how you are going to decorate—will the house have frosting "paint" or will you leave the gingerbread showing? If you are going to cover the entire house it is easier to do that first, and then put your porch roof on. It is hard to work under the roof, especially when putting wreaths or candy on the doors or walls.

For your first try you may want to paint your windows and doors on. I have seen beautiful houses done in a variety of different ways, so don't take on a more difficult design than you can do without getting frustrated! If you want to do glass windows and have open doors, you have to plan ahead for that. Glass is easy to add to your gingerbread house by following this simple recipe. Mix the following ingredients in a small saucepan:

1¼ cups granulated sugar

½ cup corn syrup

⅓ cup water

Heat these ingredients gently on medium heat, stirring constantly until the sugar dissolves. Bring to a boil, and then cook it without stirring until the temperature reaches 310 degrees.

If you want to have glass windows simply follow the recipe, and remember to plan ahead and cut your windows out in advance.

Above, beautiful glass windows with icing shutters. Below, see how the glass windows are filled before you put up your walls.

You must use a candy thermometer to measure the temperature, or you run the risk of burning the sugar. Don't forget to cut out your windows and doors when you are making the gingerbread. Place your gingerbread pieces with window cutouts on a cookie sheet, and pour the liquefied sugar slowly into the openings. Don't overfill the window; it is hard to get off the gingerbread walls. Let this cool overnight and you'll now have beautiful windows in your house. If you live in a humid area of the country and you want to have glass windows, it is a good idea to install a light inside your house. The heat from the little bulb (like the ones used for candles, or lighted ceramic houses) keeps the windows from getting sticky and also keeps the gingerbread hard. If you plan on doing this, make sure you cut a hole in your wood base before you build so that you can place the bulb inside the house when you're ready.

Now comes the part that's the most fun with your children. Look around your house for interesting items to decorate with. After a trip to a local candy store where we found sugar plum candies, we incorporated these candies by flattening them and created a blue stone walkway. For the blacktop driveway in this picture, we used crushed Oreos from which we had removed the cream beforehand.

Gingerbread houses can be your own special creation. You can make them whimsical, or in this case we were trying to replicate a dear friend's house in our historic district. We made our own pattern based on measurements given to us by the owner. If you want to try making your own pattern, expect to add another two to ten hours for drawing all of the pieces you need.

When using the tips that came with your pastry bag, try playing with different ones so you get a feel for

Be creative when you decorate, almost any candy can be incorporated into your design.

which one you'll use for a specific decoration. Practice on a piece of wax paper before you pipe the frosting onto the house. The flower tip makes nice wreaths, which you can put directly on the house, or you can pipe them onto the wax paper, let them harden, then glue them onto the house. This is also the method for porch railings and fences. Using the smallest tip, pipe the whole railing onto the wax paper, let it harden overnight, then carefully place it on your porch, or in the yard. Make some extras, since they break easily. Some other decorating ideas are black string licorice for window frames, brown licorice or chocolate bars for a roof, candy canes for posts, and green spice candies for building a pine tree. Another cute way to make trees is to use an ice cream cone as your base and, using one of the larger tips, pipe green frosting on to the cone, making branches. Practice this one first on wax

paper. Shrubs can be made the same way, using marshmallows as your base.

When your masterpiece is done, it's time to cover the base board. We make a big batch of frosting for this, because more is better! You want to make sure you get good coverage and also hide any mistakes. We usually put snow on the roof, both to hide mistakes, and so we don't have to cover the entire roof with candy.

If, after your first attempt, you find you want to become a master builder, we recommend purchasing the following book—*Making Great Gingerbread Houses*, by Aaron Morgan and Paige Gilchrist. Have Fun!

INDEX

H

I

R

S